MAN SCHOOL

Relating with Women
In the #MeToo Era

MATTHEW SOLOMON

MAN SCHOOL
Relating with Women
In the #MeToo Era

BY
MATTHEW SOLOMON

Copyright © 2018 Matthew Solomon

All rights reserved. No part of this book may be used or reproduced by any means, graphic, electronic, or mechanical, including photocopying, recording, taping or by any information storage retrieval system without the written permission of the author except in the case of brief quotations embodied in critical articles and interviews.

Because of the dynamic nature of the Internet, any web addresses or links contained in this book may have changed since publication and may no longer be valid. The views expressed in this work are solely the views of the author and do not necessarily reflect the views of the publisher, and the publisher hereby disclaims any responsibility for them.

ISBN-13: 978-1987799019
ISBN-10: 1987799011

Many special thanks to:

Navae Lukas, Jordan Ancel
& Kathryn DeHoyos

Your love, support and belief in me,
helped make all of this possible.

ACKNOWLEDGEMENTS AND GRATITUDE

Thank you for your interest in this book and for sharing it with the people you love. My sincerest intention is that it provides valuable and healing information for you, your families and the world.

As the information shared here is a product of my experiences and the lessons I have learned along the way, I wish to thank each and every one of my teachers in life up until this point.

Mom & Dad
Sadie, Spencer & Gabriel
Bella & Maya
Lisa & Cesar Mayorga
Jamie Hayes
Jerry Baden
Larry Pearson
Jerry Burkhard
Crystal Henderson
Brian Rodda
Lyn Levine
Shihan Marcello Aquinid
Laura Landry
Robert Lorenz
Angela Jones
Tolley Casparis
Maya Walker
Shannon Bobo
Thomas Hargrove

Ma & Pa
Ethel Polsky
Rabbi Steven Robbins
Lynn Rodden
Daniel Whiteside
Kathy Bosco
Manal Maurice
Judy-Lee Chen Sang
Barbara Law
Beverly Neufeld
Lucas McGough
The AKMA
Renita Gale
Amy Startari
Gurumeher Khalsa
Terry & Carrie Davis
Duane Cobb
Kate
Marianne Williamson

MAN SCHOOL

Minista Jazz
Genevieve Rackham
Lesley Tavernier
Govind Das
Lillie Claire Love
Dawn Cartwright
Chelsea Didier
Sushila Danae Battagione
Maya McClean
Tara Sindler
YOU

Jasmine Aten
Khayr Carter
Rev. Valerie Love
Dr. Erin Fall Haskell
Alison Armstrong
Erika Briones
Scott Murphy
Heather Rhea Dawn
Melanie Hirsch
Astor West
WE

GOD.

CONTENTS

Introduction   11

HOW DID WE GET HERE?

Chapter 1   Sex   15
Chapter 2   Women Are Not Men   20
Chapter 3   A Change Has Come   23
Chapter 4   The Problems   26
Chapter 5   Toxic Masculinity   35

WHAT NOW (FOR HER)?

Chapter 6   Safety   44
Chapter 7   Engaging with Her   50
Chapter 8   Listening   53
Chapter 9   Chivalry   58
Chapter 10 Tantra   60
Chapter 11 Provide   63

WHAT'S NEXT (FOR HIM)?

Chapter 12 Cultivate Your Being-ness 65

WHAT'S NEXT (FOR THE WORLD)?

Chapter 13 The Future   69

            Resources   71

MATTHEW SOLOMON

INTRODUCTION

If you are reading this, someone cared enough and thought enough about you to put this book in your hands. If you bought this for yourself, I commend you on seeking out the knowledge that will be imparted to you. In the face of "you're doing it wrong," either having heard that from someone else or believing that about yourself, you are standing for a difference, making a difference, being the difference for women, men and the future of our society.

Detailed in this book are the lessons, points of view, and ways of being that I believe, based on my experience, will make *the* difference. Maybe you have been confused by what is happening in regards to sexuality. Maybe you are already aware of what needs to be done. Maybe you just want to know that you are ok and not alone. Whatever the case may be, you are here and I acknowledge you for that.

My name is Matthew Solomon. In addition to being a coach, I am an award-winning filmmaker and a father of 3.

I have spent most of my adult life seeking the Truth; seeking ways to develop myself, communicate better, love deeper, be more effective in my life and affect change in the world.

My journey started with Judaism and moved on to Kabbalah, kinesiology, martial arts, Eastern philosophy, sociology, comparative religions, angels, crystals, Buddhism, mindfulness, meditation, yoga, astrology, Tantra, witchcraft and magick. I taught Chinese Kenpo, was an Introduction Leader and coach for Landmark Worldwide, and have studied relationships and communication with countless teachers.

It is important to note that I have always had many female friends, I was married 9 years and have been in several long-term relationships where I have worked very hard to apply what I have learned. I was in a 2-year relationship following my divorce. When that ended, I decided to just date and get to know myself, women, and what works/doesn't work for me, and what I want/don't want.

In the 18 months following that relationship, I had been on dates with over 60 women, and I have pretty much heard it all.

I am passionate about equality. My commitment is that everyone, every single person, feels heard, loved and understood. I thank you for taking this step with me.

MATTHEW SOLOMON

HOW DID WE GET HERE?

CHAPTER 1: SEX

Sex is why we are all here. Not only is it what actually brought you here into this existence, but it is probably the force behind what led you to this book. My intention is to always be inclusive. Primarily, this book will cover male/female relationships, however, there is much to be applied to all kinds of relationships and gender identities. If you identify as LGBTQ, I invite you to take in what is shared here and look for how it applies to you and your life. I am always available to you and can be reached through my website if you want to look at anything more in-depth.

(www.CoachWithMatthewSolomon.com)

In looking at sex, it is important to start with the fact that you probably know very little at this point. It is not your fault. The truth is, we have been given next to no information or training when it comes to sex and intimacy. Most of us bounce around from partner to partner, not really knowing what to do.

We have seen things in movies and online, but the fictitious depiction of the sex act is not realistic for what is pleasurable, or even do-able, for most.

The approach for most of us is to find someone we are at least attracted-enough to, and then rub our parts together until (hopefully) we both orgasm, and we are done. It is exciting at first because it is new. Then, we fall into a routine, and gradually, over time, the sex stops, the intimacy stops, and the relationship dies.

Unfortunately, like most of the really important things, we are not taught how to be intimate, how to really have sex, how to enjoy sex, or how to even navigate the ebbs and flows of relationships. This was how my journey went, perhaps your experience was similar:

When I was around 10 years old, my parents gave my 6-year-old sister and I an illustrated book that "explained" puberty, etc. I am paraphrasing here, but basically it said: "Boys have a penis and girls have a vagina. When we are young, we have no body hair. During puberty, we grow hair on our privates and underarms. Girls develop breasts and menstruate. When a boy becomes aroused, his penis gets erect/hard. When aroused, and when choosing to make a baby, he lays close enough to her so that his penis goes inside her vagina. She gets pregnant and 9 months later, they have a baby."

At 10, I remember thinking, "My what goes where? How!?" I asked my dad how it worked, and he said, "You put it in." Then I asked what it feels like, to which he responded, "I don't know, it's exciting." As a 10-year-old boy, my version of "exciting" was what I felt being on a rollercoaster or riding my bike really fast!

I imagined that as my dad's "excited" face with him laying on top of my mom. This vision of sex looked like the weirdest, goofiest, and most awkward thing to me. There was no love, no connection, no *intimacy.* It was a chore.

Of course, sex was talked about by kids in school who were always claiming they were having it, even in 5th and 6th grade. Sex Ed in elementary and middle school was basically: "Don't do it. But if you do it, wear a condom because you're either going to get pregnant or die." Fun!!! How inspiring! It seemed scary as hell and yet, of course everyone said they wanted to do it or were already doing it.

Interestingly, masturbation was considered something to be ashamed of. We boys would make fun of each other with accusations of "jacking off." So, we *shouldn't* practice, we don't know what to do, and then we fumble around and hope for the best. Meanwhile, everyone in the movies looks like they have it all together, and anyone who claimed to be sexually active talked a good game as well. Truth be told, I was a virgin until I was 21 or 22. I was afraid, I never thought I would measure up, and so I never pursued sex.

If you are a man reading this who has not had the best sex life, you are not alone! Know this. And know that from the many women I have discussed these topics with, good male lovers are in the minority. The really good news is, there is so much more available through sex than you can even imagine! As you move forward with understanding, with what you will learn here, you can create a powerful new paradigm of intimacy. In addition to heightened states of passion and arousal, you can actually manifest and create things with sex—and not just babies. I will get into that a little later.

CHAPTER 2: WOMEN ARE NOT MEN

Sounds obvious, right? You would think so, however, most of the ineffective interactions I witness between men and women involve men trying to fit women into their male constructs. "I don't get it, I wouldn't do it that way!" "I'm afraid of things but I wouldn't let that stop me!" "You have nothing to be afraid of, that would never happen [to me]!"

That would never happen TO ME.

Men and women have obvious physical differences. Men are generally larger in stature, broader shoulders, taller, etc. Women are generally smaller in stature, wider hips, smaller bones, etc. Ironically, we appear different, and yet even with that difference in appearance, we expect each other to behave the same. How is that? Alison Armstrong, the founder of PAX Programs, Inc. (a leader in the education of understanding men and women), reminds women that *"a man is not a hairy woman."*

Men are wired differently, have different dispositions, different ways of handling things, a different type of focus, etc. And so, to the men reading this book, a woman is not a pretty man with breasts. They are wired differently, have different societal experiences, different ways of handling things, a different type of focus, and honestly, a different role.

Look at it this way: a woman creates life. She has the ability to grow life inside of her. She bonds with that life very differently than a man. She is equipped to feed and nurture that life for quite some time. Women are built differently. Their bodies go through cycles that cause changes *every month*. Their hormones act and react in support of those cycles.

We as men, cannot relate to women like we relate to ourselves. She has a very different chemical make-up…and *very different experience of the world than we do.* So, as you continue through this book, I invite you to read, listen and observe from a neutral place. YOUR WAY IS NOT THE RIGHT WAY FOR A WOMAN. What works for you will not work for her. Let that go right now.

Honestly, one of the very best things you can do for a woman is hear her experience and simply get it and acknowledge it. Don't argue, don't try and fix it, just get it. And breathe…

CHAPTER 3: A CHANGE HAS COME

Clearly, something is different now. There has been a cultural shift, which may be why you are reading this book. Women have had enough, are fed up and have found their voice. If you have not been aware of their societal struggles up until now, this may have blind-sided you. The #metoo movement, the #timesup movement, and the sarcastic hash-tag #notallmen have been born from this shift. Because I know that there are men who do not know and/or do not understand these movements, I will explain:

#MeToo was adopted as the hashtag of women coming out to share their stories of rape, sexual harassment, manipulation, molestation and more by family members, trusted adults, random attackers, bosses, co-workers, etc. With social media giving a broad audience to women sharing their experiences following the "grab 'em by the pussy" statements of Donald Trump,

and continuing into other high-profile cases involving a growing list of celebrities, women who were voicing their fears and experiences, initially found unifying power in this.

A great many men simply had no idea that all of this even existed in such great numbers. Personally, even knowing how prevalent these occurrences are, seeing my entire Facebook feed filled with #metoo posts stopped me in my tracks as well, and brought about so much sadness. Pretty much every single woman I am friends with online posted a #metoo experience.

#TimesUp followed #metoo by representing the raising legal funds to fight back against abusers, while simultaneously putting men on notice that this behavior was not going to be tolerated any more. I am including *#notallmen* because it is relevant to this discussion and points to how men have dismissed and talked-down to women, by asserting themselves as "more knowledgeable" (a practice known as "*mansplaining*").

Unfortunately, as women began to unify and share their horrific experiences, often times a man would insert a comment along the lines of "well, not all men are like that." Men would also argue that perhaps her version of what happened, wasn't what actually happened, or that "she must have done something wrong to have that happen." In fact, just the other day a woman was describing her fear of walking down the street, to which a man said "I'm not afraid, there's nothing to be afraid of." I will address this more later, but what he did was exactly the wrong thing: asserting that his way works for her and dismissing her fear based on HER ACTUAL LIFE EXPERIENCES.

The change has come. Women have found their voice, have found each other and are no longer willing to tolerate the behavior that has victimized, objectified and terrorized them.

CHAPTER 4: THE PROBLEMS

As I shared earlier, in around a month-and-a-half's time, I went on dates with over 60 women. I was on several dating sites, read their profiles which often contained complaints about men's behavior, and I listened to their horror stories. Women friends of mine on Facebook would also laboriously share how they were being harassed on public posts and in private messages—often receiving un-wanted dick-pics. I would see a friend post a heart-felt biographical account in writing or as a video, only to have some guy comment "nice boobs." Many complaints, besides dick pics, are that random men send private messages just saying "hi" or "hey." These women regularly ask me, "what is that?!? What is wrong with these guys?"

Perhaps it's a numbers thing, perhaps you were just shy and didn't know what to say, perhaps you were taught that's what you are supposed to do, or maybe that's your version of "giving it a shot," but it doesn't work.

And while you may get a response on very rare occasions, it is really not an effective way to open up a conversation with a woman, especially a stranger who has not invited this from you. It is actually creepy from the perspective of the women who have commented on this type of activity. It shows no honor or respect for the woman you are attempting to communicate with. Trust me, putting just a little bit of thought into a message, introducing yourself and saying "hello," will go a long way. Please get that this message must also be sent with the understanding she does not owe you a response and she may decline. You get to be ok with that. You MUST be ok with that.

Another bit of crucial information is that WOMEN ARE AFRAID. Again, they have been objectified, harassed, attacked, bullied, raped, molested, disrespected, etc. for centuries, with no real repercussions for their attackers. Last year, there was a viral video of a woman walking around the streets of New York for several hours one day showing the relentless cat-calls, comments, random guys following her, and more.

Men think this behavior should be received as a compliment...IT IS NOT AND IT IS FUCKING SCARY FOR THEM!

Here are just some of the reasons women feel fear around men:

> Men have considerably more testosterone than women, making our potential to generate the power to hurt and do harm, scary. They see a potential for out-of-control rage in us. We express our anger outwardly. And we tend to be physically stronger in a way that would over-power most women. Even the smallest man can generate enough rage to scare the shit out of a woman. It is not a size thing, it is an intensity thing. It is an inherently *chemical* thing.
>
> Men, in our current society, have advantages (privileges) that women do not. Men are predominantly, and historically, the law-makers, the law-enforcers, the controllers of money, the controllers of property and the deciders of what rights a woman can have.

Common phrases such as: "A woman's place is in the home" or "a woman needs to listen to her man," and "she had it coming," are all ingrained at this point. "Look at the way she was dressed," is another one.

Women have expressed to me that men rarely come to the aid of a woman in distress at the hands of another man, because they "don't want to rock the boat," "don't want to get involved," and hope things will de-escalate by themselves. I have heard recent stories of: a woman being assaulted in a club with no one jumping in, a girlfriend of a friend being date-raped and not reporting it because "it won't make a difference," and another woman almost being raped by a restaurant manager—she escaped but refused to say who it was and report it because, again, "it won't make a difference."

Music, movies, television, history, and pornography all support this attitude. "Women are supposed to be subservient and know their place."

The woman is "battered," not "the man is an animal." And just to drive the point home, this is what has been normalized:

> "I moved on her like a bitch, but I couldn't get there, and she was married. Then all of a sudden I see her, she's now got the big phony tits and everything. I'm automatically attracted to beautiful [women]—I just start kissing them. It's like a magnet. Just kiss. I don't even wait. And when you're a star they let you do it. You can do anything ... Grab them by the pussy. You can do anything."

This is the product of generations of INDOCTRINATION. So, how did we get here? There are so many examples I can point to that show how this sort of thing was made "ok." I was a child in the 70s, a teen in the 80s and a young adult in the 90s. I do not have to look any further than the art and culture of those times to illustrate how women have been objectified and put at-risk.

Before I get in to this, please know that I am not a prudish man calling for the burning of books, records and CDs.

I am a product of that generation and grew up on the music, movies and imagery. This isn't a make-wrong, and it's not like I will never listen to Van Halen or Snoop Dogg again. This is my assessment of how we got to this place.

SEX SELLS! Van Halen, Motley Crüe, Poison and countless others birthed the "music video girl": the good girl turned stripper that was the prize for their success. The songs were about hunting girls and getting laid with the more the better. Their videos showed the band members at parties surrounded by many women, sometimes leaving as the next fresh group of women entered the room for the entertainment of the guys in the band. And if one of the women got out of hand, she was removed as her replacement promptly arrived.

The messages were that women are bountiful, expendable and exist as a trophy for the man. If you look at Rap Music and videos, it is more of the same. "Bitches and Hos." "We don't give a fuck about hos."

Again, women are bountiful, expendable and exist purely for the pleasure of men. It is necessary for men to be loyal to each other, but not to a woman: "Bros before hos." And the thing about the music industry is that this behavior is beyond expected...it has been a *requirement*. At least the portrayal has been a requirement.

And then there are the movies. All of our beloved "coming of age" films (i.e., "Porky's," "Revenge of the Nerds," and even sweet, heartfelt movies like "Sixteen Candles") are filled with the same types of messages. "Porky's" follows a group of high school boys on a quest to see naked women and get laid for the first time. "Revenge of the Nerds" adds the underdog twist: The jocks who get the hottest girls on campus are assholes to the nerds who are just wanting to be accepted.

The nerds use their superior intelligence to install spy cameras in the girl's sorority house (to see them naked) and the head nerd even disguises himself to trick the main hot girl into having sex with him (resulting in her being very pleasantly surprised).

Even the love story of "Sixteen Candles" includes a scene where The Geek borrows Samantha's underwear to show off to his friends and win "cool" points.

In fact, another horrific exchange comes when Jake hands his passed-out girlfriend over to The Geek to drive her home after doing whatever he wants with her. "She won't even remember," he says. "Just make sure you get her home," he says. She wakes up the next morning in the car with The Geek, not knowing what happened, but somehow very sexually satisfied.

The messages:

- Boys crave sex and good girls do not.
- The "promiscuous" (popular girls) are mean and deserve whatever is coming to them.
- Girls need to be tricked into having sex.
- Girls need to be drunk or drugged to have sex.

- A girl's sex is the trophy, the notch on the headboard, the rite of passage.
- Girls/women exist solely for the enjoyment of boys/men.

Which leads us to "*Toxic Masculinity...*"

CHAPTER 5: TOXIC MASCULINITY

This hot-button term has stirred up quite a bit of anger in men. What is "Toxic Masculinity?" In short, it is a condition of *entitlement* felt by men in this male-dominated society. A few examples of how this is expressed are the previously-mentioned "mansplaining," "infantilizing," and the concept of the "Friend Zone," based on the belief that women exist for the pleasure of men. This is toxic, because it perpetuates an unhealthy and unsafe environment. Toxic, because it diminishes everything that women have to offer. Toxic, because it poisons our relationships with everyone.

When confronted by the accusation of being a toxic male, a tactic of some men is to respond by labeling themselves as "Alpha Males," flexing their muscles in a way that is intended to impose their dominance. What it really does is get a collective eye-roll from those around them who know the difference.

I wrote a Facebook post addressing this on March 18, 2018:

> *I see a lot of people confusing "Alpha Male" and "Asshole Male" these days. There is a difference.*
>
> *ASSHOLE MALE: "Fuck you and fuck your feelings." "This is me whether you like it or not (and I'm saying this because deep down, I really, REALLY care what you think of me, so I am just going to be louder to cover that up)." "You're a whiny 'lil bitch when you should just be impressed with my abs." "How dare you say 'no' to me...I'm an Alpha Male!" He imposes his opinions and tells you what you should and shouldn't do whether you ask for it or not. He demands respect to feed and protect his ego, etc.*
>
> *ALPHA MALE: Leads by example, creates and inspires people to become leaders, inspires others by who he is being, considers what is best for all before acting, IS respected and never feels the need to declare that he is an Alpha.*

The following are just a few examples of Toxic Masculinity being expressed:

"Well, actually...". The words that make every woman cringe. Why? Because they are almost always followed by a man's attempt to assert his dominance and prove a woman wrong. You think you are being helpful. You think you are "just setting the record straight." What you are doing is undermining and belittling her, and ALL WOMEN. I have seen these assertions everywhere: not only on posts or in conversations of an emotional nature, but regarding a woman's appearance, presentation, and even a woman's business.

A dear friend, who is a very successful healer, had a man who knows nothing about her profession attempt to school her on her rates and business structure. Even if he knew something about her business, which he did not, *she didn't ask.*

Here's the thing: We, as men, use each other as counsel. We bounce ideas off of each other. We come to each other for advice. The difference is, we *request* the counsel, ideas and advice from each other. The guys that walk around telling us what we should or shouldn't do when we haven't asked them, are assholes. Am I right? This is how we are with each other and yet, with women, we have been conditioned to insert ourselves into their business, thereby becoming the assholes. And it does not matter what your intention is. If your opinion is not asked for, it is not wanted. We do this with each other, we need to do this with women.

"Infantilizing" is another issue. What do I mean by this? Calling a woman whom you are not in a relationship with: "cutie," "sweetie," "honey," "darling," baby," etc. It is perceived as condescending and it again asserts male-dominance. Even if it is not your intention to have her feel that way, why would you choose to call her by any of those things in the first place? If it is an attempt to win her over, or have her lower her guard or feel safe, know that this is not effective, and is quite offensive.

"The Friend Zone" also needs to be addressed. I have been guilty of using this entitlement-influenced label myself. What is this and why do we need to stop using it? I mentioned before that I have always had many female friends in my life. In addition to getting along with women, the truth is that I was afraid and insecure romantically. I was afraid of asking someone out for fear of being rejected and, as I got older, I was afraid that my lack of experience would lead to more rejection and embarrassment. So, I had friends who were women, many of whom I was very attracted to, and found myself relegated to "The Friend Zone."

This culturally-created *prison of failure* would be my home. What did it mean? It meant that I was less of a man because I couldn't "score chicks." It meant that I was less of a man because I was "shy," or "weak," or "not Alpha enough." It meant that I "had no game." It meant that I was a pussy. All of that meaning wrapped up into a fictitious construct based on the premise that "women are here as objects for men."

The veil was lifted for me about a year ago:

> *I was on a 3rd date with a woman who I liked very much. I was feeling all the feels, I had become comfortable with courting and initiating, and had worked hard on my relationship and intimacy skills. I was no longer the man I was at 13, or 24, or 30 years old. So, I had developed confidence and was comfortable flowing intimately. This woman seemed to possess all the qualities I had been looking for, except something was missing: she just was not feeling me in that way.*
>
> *My insecurity reared its head, and in a moment of awkwardness, I said to her, "Please don't put me in the friend zone." This really kind and gracious woman turned to me and asked, "Why wouldn't you want to be my friend?" And I got it: chemistry is chemistry.*

I have certainly been on the other side of that conversation, where a woman was interested in me and I was not feeling it with her. There wasn't anything wrong, there wasn't anything wrong with me, and it had been incredibly objectifying to measure my self-worth against if she wanted to sleep with me or not.

Lastly, I need to address the influence of...PORN:

Let me start by saying that I have friends who have worked in porn. I respect the actors and wish them the best. That being said, pornography has greatly flawed the ideas of sex and intimacy with its violent and unrealistic portrayal of what sex "should look like." A man shows up at the door, answered by a hot girl. He may or may not be attractive, it doesn't matter, but he has a large penis. She gets one look and HAS to have him right then and there. He pounds away, she moans and screams and then he ejaculates, usually on her face. Nothing special. Nothing intimate. Nothing worth connecting with someone over.

Generations of boys have grown up watching this, thinking this is how it is supposed to be, and that this is what women want...and when it's not like that, and when women aren't satisfied, shame shows up and intimacy and love are killed. Men, because we have very little opportunity to openly share with each other, internalize our shame or act out in anger. The really sad thing is, porn has "devolved" to become even more violent and degrading towards women. Not only are kids not being educated (as I was not), the depictions are way more extreme and way more available (thanks to the internet).

Along with the notion that women exist only for the pleasure of men, comes the belief that men do not need to court women or do *anything* for the women in their lives. Men have not been taught to ask women out, opting for "let's hang out" instead of "may I take you on a date?" Even "Netflix and Chill" is passive, in my opinion. Men have not been taught to be clear with their intentions and women are left not-knowing, which is un-settling and frustrating for them.

So, what now?

WHAT NOW? (FOR HER)

CHAPTER 6: SAFETY

What do women want? THEY WANT TO FEEL SAFE! A big part of a woman feeling safe includes having the experience of being heard, understood and loved. For them to be free to express themselves in the ways that feel good to them. This may involve dressing in ways that some would judge as "provocative." It may include dancing, or just jogging down the street in normal workout clothes *without* being harassed. I have seen many men try to diminish, deny and explain away the fear women have and why they feel unsafe. I want to share with you an experience I had in a PAX seminar I attended, lead by Alison Armstrong:

> *It is the first day of the seminar and Alison is discussing this same subject (safety). She asked the men in the room, "How many of you have felt afraid for your lives in the last year?" Several hands went up.*

"How many of you have felt afraid for your lives in the last 6 months?" Most of the hands went down. "The last month?" ALL hands went down. "The last week?" None.

Then she asked the women, "How many of you have felt afraid for your lives in the last year?" Every single hand went up. "The last 6 months?" Every single hand stayed up. "The last month?" The majority of hands stayed up. "The last week?" Quite a few hands were still up. "What about today? How many of you have been afraid for your lives today?" Around 15-20 hands stayed up and it was only 11AM.

So, here's the thing: we can try and rationalize this all we want. We can judge women all we want. We can offer up what we think they should or should not do, wear or should not wear, in any given situation, but it won't change a thing. We, as men, need to understand that this is what women experience. Period. Nothing we say will change that. What we can do is *listen* and *understand.* What we get to do, now that we understand, is create the space that has them feel safe.

Knowing the fear a woman likely feels in certain situations, you can carry yourself in a way that lets her know you are not a threat. You can choose not to approach her if it seems inappropriate or if it may be uncomfortable for her. It isn't about you. It isn't about your ego or self-worth. As an honorable man of integrity, YOU get to provide that space for her, finally.

I had a Facebook discussion with a man recently who said he was trying to navigate attempting a relationship with a co-worker, but avoid being accused of sexual harassment. The woman whose thread it was, and I, offered many suggestions for how he could approach her in a safe and respectful way; the most powerful being to state that his intention was to take her out on a date. He would not hear that and was stuck on how he could seduce (manipulate) her into bed. When I asked what he could do to make her feel safe regardless of the outcome, he could not see past attempts at trickery.

This is a big reason women do not trust men currently. We always seem to be "up to something." There always seems to be a motive—because there usually is.

Several women I have dated shared with me that they thought I was extremely kind, but were on-guard because they had been tricked before by men that *seemed* kind.

Women do not have many safe options on how to deal with men, either.

> A woman I know went out to a bar recently to watch a baseball game. She just wanted to watch the game and not be bothered, but knew this was not possible. She even dressed-down, and yet, was continuously approached and hit-on. She would say she had a boyfriend and it would not deter them. She would politely decline a drink and be subjected to, "What, you think you're too good for me bitch?!?" She would half-listen and half-ignore, hoping he would lose interest.

> I asked her why she didn't just say "Fuck off" or "Go away?" Her response, *"Because then they might get mad and you never know what they will do."*

She said that many times, she had been followed home after interactions like this. Two "nice-seeming" guys offered to walk her home from the bar. She accepted, but pretended her home was two blocks away from where she actually lived.

This also occurs relentlessly online. As I mentioned before, the random "hi," "hello," and dick pics that flood women's private messages are often followed by angry, degrading and hurtful comments if she does not respond graciously. A woman friend posted a video about her healing practice and it was a really beautiful and heartfelt video. The first comment was a guy saying, "sexy and slutty" followed by "nice boobs." This was on a public video regarding her business (not that it should make a difference), and yet this happens all the time. So, understand this, when you are commenting, approaching and initiating, you are one of a long line of others who most-likely have been complete assholes to her already. Her guard is up and justifiably so.

So, how, when and where are we able to approach women?

CHAPTER 7: ENGAGING WITH HER

Anything can be done with anyone, anywhere and anytime. The key is to read the situation, read the other person, and be respectful. First of all, please, please, PLEASE get rid of the "How to Pick Up Chicks" books and programs that you see advertised. Those are all based on manipulation and designed to appeal to the lowest-common denominator, making a woman a notch on your headboard vs a living, breathing, beautiful being.

Genuine, heartfelt interactions go much further, and if you are willing to be real and authentic, you have a much better chance at success. Again, understanding that most women get harassed constantly, receive weird messages all the time, and are going to be on guard, you get to embody your role as a safe, stable, man of integrity.

I invite you to grab a notebook and brainstorm for a few minutes. Ask yourself: *"what are things I can do to approach her in a way that has her feel safe and respected?"*

I honestly think that the reason most men just send a "hi" or a "hey" is because they expect to be rejected and figure if they at least send that, then mayyyyybe she will respond. Some men will even send several "hi"s and then get mad when she does not reply. So, coming from a place of making her feel safe and respected, don't you think it would be more effective to simply say *"Hi! I have really been enjoying your posts and wanted to say hello!"* or something like that?

Again, it is important to be especially considerate if this is happening on Facebook or another social platform as opposed to a dating site. The benefit of being on a dating site, is that there is already an understanding that she will be contacted. In that case, saying something about her profile that caught your eye would be a good way to initiate a conversation. Putting thought and consideration into any and all interactions with a woman will have her be more open and relaxed, whether she responds or not.

The same goes with walking down the street or standing in line for coffee.

A simple smile and "hello" creates an open and safer space. If you aren't trying to pick her up, she can relax. And if you are a man who puts women at ease, women will enjoy being around you. And when they are around you, one of the greatest gifts you can give them, is to listen...

CHAPTER 8: LISTENING

This is the holy grail right here and THE KEY TO SUCCESS in any relationship: *The Art of Listening!*

Realize that in any conversation, there are multiple dialogues going on all at once; there are the words you are saying and the words she is saying, then there are the thoughts you are having about what she is saying, and the thoughts she is having about what you are saying. In any given conversation, there are at least 4 dialogues going on simultaneously! How can anyone be expected to hear and retain anything under those circumstances? There is a technique I use that has 4 steps, and it has me be so present with whomever I am conversing with, that they feel heard and understood. When you are doing the following technique, the thing that will make it easier, and more effective, is eye-contact. Maintain eye-contact, give her your full attention and remember to breathe as you apply the following 4 steps:

1. ***Give up the need to be right:*** Most of the time when we are "listening," we are actually just preparing what we are going to say next. We are preparing because we have a position, a point of view about something, and there is an underlying fear that we will need to defend it. We listen to her from our point of view, which does not have us connect with her. So, forget about being right. Nothing bad will happen if you are wrong. *Especially if you are willing to be wrong.* Giving up the need to be right, opens the door for you to be present and hear her.

2. ***Retain the words she is saying.*** Being able to repeat back word-for-word what she has shared with you, keeps you engaged with her. The common mistake made by men is thinking this is all you need to do. The classic example is, *"Of course I am listening, you said _____."* Being able to repeat exactly what she said is a start; however, it is not sufficient to her, or anyone for that matter, on its own.

Honestly, we can hear words and recite them pretty easily. It is the next step that makes the difference.

3. *Acknowledge her experience.*
Or said another way, *GET HOW SHE FEELS.* Women are feeling beings. They are open and sensitive, they are connected to their emotions, they are intuitive. Women generally communicate from their feelings, and so the more you can pick up on, and reflect their feelings back to them, the more they will feel heard, understood and loved.

It might look something like this:

> Her (sharing about her day): *"I had a meeting and everyone was so disorganized and nothing got done. Then I went for coffee and the barista screwed up my order and so I just gave up!"*

You (listening for her experience/ how she felt): *"Wow! That sounds so frustrating! You must've been losing your shit!"*

That little bit of acknowledgement will have her feel heard, understood and loved. The next step will take it even deeper:

4. **Listening for her commitment.** When there is an upset, it is because there is an unfulfilled commitment. Meaning, she wanted something to happen a certain way and for a certain reason, and it did not. In the example above, her commitment may have been around things going smoothly and efficiently. And what that might sound like coming from you is: *"I can tell you just really wanted everyone to be prepared so things would go smoothly, and when it didn't, you just needed some comfort, didn't you?"*

Putting it all together would be like: *"Wow! That sounds so frustrating! You must've been losing your shit! I mean, I know you just wanted everyone to be prepared so things would go smoothly, and when that didn't happen, you wanted that comforting latte, and that didn't happen either! I am so sorry!"*

With this technique, she gets that you get her, and that has her feel safe. It really is one of the most loving things you can do for a woman, and she will appreciate it.

CHAPTER 9: CHIVALRY

While the concept of "chivalry" originated in 10th Century AD France as a code of morals for the battlefield, the term has become associated with ways that men can express their respect for women through certain actions. What many women point to as a lost art, is a practice that goes a long way. Women are, unfortunately, not used to being honored/taken care of. I do this, not because I am "stronger" or "dominant," but because I honor her as the Divine Feminine.

Women are to be nurtured and taken care of. I have always practiced this, and a coach of mine who has always done the same, told me that he always makes it clear to any woman he is with: *"You don't touch any doors. I got them."* Understand: THIS IS NOT SEXIST. The intention of this is not to diminish the woman at all. The intention is to honor her, have her feel safe and cherished. OF COURSE, she is totally capable of opening a car door. But she shouldn't have to!

She is a woman: the creator of life, the birther of projects, the natural-born manifestor! And she deserves to be treated like the QUEEN that she is. So:

- Open doors for her
- Wait to start eating until she does
- Give her your coat if she is cold
- Let her pass through doors first
- Carry her bags
- She orders first and/or you order for her
- Check in with her to see what she needs
- Hold her hand or have your hand on her back as you cross the street
- Watch for her safety
- And more!

Google "chivalry." Watch old Humphrey Bogart movies. Pay attention to how a man cherishes and shows appreciation for a woman.

CHAPTER 10: TANTRA

As my late, great Jazz Guitar instructor Joe Diorio used to say in his thick Chicagoan accent when he was teaching at the University of Southern California in the early 90s: *"This is the shit right here, gentlemen."* Tantra, like chivalry, is another practice that dates back many centuries and whose meaning and application has evolved over time. Primarily associated with sex, sex magick, sex rituals, and hedonism, Tantra is so much more, and at the same time, much simpler than that. It is a way of being in life. It is a life-style. It is connection. Tantra is acceptance.

Western culture loves to pervert sex and anything related. As such, most miss the true beauty of what sex can be. In practicing Tantra, you learn to connect, truly connect, with another being, in a way in which the two of you become one unified, fluid energy.

This energy can stay between the both of you, or you can amplify out. What is really incredible is that, when this is done and this state of connection is reached, everything that is not love, melts away. All resistance, insecurity, anger, resentment, judgement, fear of being judged, disappears as you look into the eyes of the person in front of you creating love and acceptance of you, and you mirroring that back to her. This may not make sense as written words, but if you have ever experienced this, you know what I am talking about. Actually, if you sit in front of a mirror, you can create this for yourself! Gaze lovingly at the being in the mirror; love your goodness, love your flaws, love the lines in your face, love who you are and who you potentially can become.

Your willingness to create this connection with nothing else wanted or required, will provide so much space for her to feel herself, express herself and appreciate you. We create the space for them to relax and BE, and they heal us with their love and gratitude. I mentioned way back in Chapter 1 that sex can be used for manifesting.

In this connected, heightened state, with your combined intention radiating out, she (the creator of life) amplifies this and "things" get created. You are the foundation for her radiation.

I recently participated in a Tantra course led by Dawn Cartwright. This course was attended by couples and singles, and Dawn's strong suggestion was that none of the singles date each other while in the course. This gift of being in a delicious space, leaving it at that and not having to take things further for the 7-week course, provided and incredible space for being, learning, acceptance and respect. I have heard the argument so many times that a man's biology requires him to pursue a woman whether she invites him and desires that, or not. Many men claim that "the pull is so strong that it cannot be diverted." This exercise I mentioned, puts that argument to rest. We can, because we choose to, MASTER OUR BIOLOGY. *It is just a question of if we want to.*

CHAPTER 11: PROVIDE

We have been taught for generations that a man's role is to "be the provider" *financially.* We have used this as a way to dominate, we have used this as a way to control, and we have also used this as a way to shame ourselves when we have not measured up in our bank accounts. So, as you can see from reading this book, there are so many more ways the we can provide and contribute. There are so many opportunities that go beyond just "bringing home the bacon" or buying dinner. Providing a safe space, a listening, intimacy, and an overall environment that honors her and has her thrive, is what is needed now.

MATTHEW SOLOMON

WHAT NOW?
(FOR HIM)

CHAPTER 12: CULTIVATE YOUR BEINGNESS

Now that you have a clearer idea of what women have been dealing with and what they need, you have a choice to make: WHO DO YOU DESIRE TO BE? What kind of a man will you be? What will you provide for her, for you, and ultimately for the world? It is my opinion that there is no one stronger than a man who knows himself and stands by his convictions and holds integrity, honor and respect as his ideals. There is a discipline, a command and mastery of yourself that is so greatly needed. I have found this for myself through the martial arts. I spent close to 14 years learning, studying, deepening and then teaching the Warrior Spirit. To be able to create space, hold space and do what is right makes a man that can be counted on. I have also reached great depths, and heights, through yoga, tai-chi and meditation. What works for you? Where do you get your inspiration? Who are the men you admire and what practices do they hold dear? YOU get to choose who you will become, and then step into that.

You get to become that safe space. Become sensual. Slow down. Give. The Samurai were not only trained in fighting, they also developed their artistic and healing abilities. These warriors of the past acknowledged the need for healing in addition to killing. You can provide for her in so many ways by holding that safe space and by knowing how to touch her. Learn to dance. Learn the art of sensual massage. Learn Tantra. Become a gift to her. Become a real gift, not the entitled *"gift"* she has encountered many times before you.

I mentioned this before: learn to do things without requiring anything in return! Women, in American culture, give and give and do and do. If you are someone that gives to her without requiring her to do anything, she can relax into her feminine bliss and rejuvenate. A woman you have cherished and nurtured will be so grateful to you! Imagine what it would be like to give her a deep and loving sensual massage without any pressure for sex? And what do you think it would be like for her to orgasm without her having to DO anything, or to "return the favor?"

I invite you to start considering HER pleasure. Start asking her, "What would make a difference for you today? What can I do for you? What may *provide* for you?"

MATTHEW SOLOMON

WHAT NOW?
(FOR THE WORLD)

CHAPTER 13: THE FUTURE

Now that you have this information, understanding, and hopefully a commitment to healing, where do you go from here? BE YOU! Be the greatest version of you that you can! Follow your curiosity, discover new things, develop, deepen, go after what you want in life! You get to lead and teach, ESPECIALLY BY EXAMPLE. And you get to be the warrior of change that leads the way for generations to come. I appreciate you. They appreciate you. Together we can do this.

Thank you so much for reading and sharing this book! I invite you to visit: www.TheManSchoolBook.com for more information, resources and the **"Man School Online Course!"**

I am always standing for your greatness!

Matthew

MATTHEW SOLOMON

RESOURCES

Out of my commitment to you, and in appreciation for your generosity in taking the time to investigate ways to heal and improve your relationships, I am happy to provide the following as resources for you to further your education:

TheManSchoolBook.com - For more information, teachings and the *"Man School Online Course."*

UnderstandMen.com - Alison Armstrong's programs for men and women. Men: be sure to check out *"The Queen's Code Challenge: Understanding Women."*

LandmarkWorldwide.com - These extraordinary programs, beginning with the Landmark Forum, have made a profound difference in my life, my relationships, and my ability to listen.

DawnCartwright.com - Explore all levels of Tantra.

LillieClaireLove.com - Master Men's Retreat

LesleyTavernier.com - While her website is geared towards women, I can tell you first-hand that she is an extraordinary healer for men as well.

ErikaBriones.com - One of the most-committed healers I have ever met.

SiriusElevation.com – T.A. Hargrove: intimacy coach and restorative healer.

TheMagicofPsalm.com – This non-profit, tax-exempt charitable organization, brings a comprehensive, creative and connected approach to sex education and wellness training.

And of course:

CoachWithMatthewSolomon.com - I am available to support you in all areas of your life. I consistently facilitate major breakthroughs for my one-on-one and group coaching clients, resulting in your re-connection to yourself, as a powerful and unstoppable force in the world.

Made in the USA
Middletown, DE
21 June 2018